Bergamasco Sheph

Bergamasco Shepherd T

Tracker & Workbook.

Includes: Bergamasco Shepherd Multi-Level Tricks, Games & Agility.

Part 1

Training Central

Copyright © 2017

All rights reserved. Without limiting rights under the copyright reserved above, no part of this publication may be reproduced, stored, introduced into a retrieval system, distributed or transmitted in any form or by any means, including without limitation photocopying, recording, or other electronic or mechanical methods, without the prior written permission of the publisher, except in the case of brief quotations embodied in critical reviews and certain other non-commercial uses permitted by copyright law.

The scanning, uploading, and/or distribution of this document via the internet or via any other means without the permission of the publisher is illegal and is punishable by law. Please purchase only authorized editions and do not participate in or encourage electronic piracy of copyrightable materials.

Introductory Note

Welcome to this interactive tricks workbook.

We want to start by thanking all of the Bergamasco Shepherd fans out there whom inspired us to complete this three part series in which we cover a variety of tricks and games that you can teach your pooch.

Our intention is for you to learn and grow with your beloved pup whilst having a great time. We trust that you will enjoy and benefit from the use of the books in this series.

Be sure to make notes on the pages found after each trick. We found this supports learning significantly.

Have fun whilst you log and note down your progress, any new ideas, thoughts, techniques that work for you/new methods, or even sketches.

Good luck and wishing you all the best.

Table of Contents

Recognize His Own Name

This is a basic trick which will teach your Bergamasco Shepherd how to react to his name.

1. When your Bergamasco Shepherd looks at you, give him a treat. Repeat this step a few times.
2. Now say your Bergamasco Shepherd's name just before you give him a treat. Repeat until your Bergamasco Shepherd learns to look at you every time you call his name.
3. As your pooch progresses, first call his name and when he looks at you, give him a treat.

How did you get on? *What challenges did you face & how did you overcome them?* What could you do better for next time? **Any new discoveries?** Funny moments? *Memorable Photos?* **Sketches?**

Any other thoughts, comments or feedback

Sit

Teach your Bergamasco Shepherd to sit when commanded to do so. This will be a useful cue for other tricks.

1. Wait for your Bergamasco Shepherd to sit.
2. When he sits, give him a treat.
3. Repeat these steps whenever your Bergamasco Shepherd sits down. Give him a treat only when he sits, not before. It will take some time for your Bergamasco Shepherd to make a connection between the treat and his sitting down. Take breaks and shorten training sessions.
4. When you notice that your Bergamasco Shepherd has reached the stage when he has learned that whenever he sits down, he will get a reward, move on to the next step.
5. Now, when your Bergamasco Shepherd sits, say the command "Sit" and give him a treat. Repeat several times, giving enough time for your Bergamasco Shepherd to associate the command with the action of sitting down.
6. Say the command, and when your Bergamasco Shepherd reacts accordingly, give him a treat.

How did you get on? *What challenges did you face & how did you overcome them?* What could you do better for next time? **Any new discoveries?** Funny moments? *Memorable Photos?* **Sketches?**

Any other thoughts, comments or feedback

Release

This trick will teach your Bergamasco Shepherd that when commanded, he is allowed to move or walk around freely, or that he has performed a trick well and he is now free to do something else.

1. Give your Bergamasco Shepherd the cue to sit.

2. Wait for a few seconds.

3. Give the command of "Release" and make a hand gesture of your choice to give a visual cue to your Bergamasco Shepherd. If you act enthusiastically, he will immediately release.

4. Reward your Bergamasco Shepherd and repeat this training until he learns to react immediately to your command and visual cue.

5. For the next session, command your Bergamasco Shepherd to sit and wait for a few seconds.

6. Without the visual cue, tell your Bergamasco Shepherd to "Release" but keep your voice energetic as though you are at the beginning of the session.

7. Reward him when he performs well.

8. When your Bergamasco Shepherd reacts accordingly to your command, move onto the final training sessions.

9. Tell your Bergamasco Shepherd to sit and wait for up to a minute (you can gradually extend this time).

10. Give him a subtle command of "Release".

11. When he reacts promptly to your command, praise him and give a generous reward.

How did you get on? *What challenges did you face & how did you overcome them?* What could you do better for next time? **Any new discoveries?** Funny moments? *Memorable Photos?* **Sketches?**

Any other thoughts, comments or feedback

Stay

These steps will teach your Bergamasco Shepherd to stay in one place until you release him.

1. Command your Bergamasco Shepherd to sit and then give him a treat.
2. Tell your Bergamasco Shepherd to stay, wait for just a few seconds, say "Release" and then give him a treat.
3. Tell your Bergamasco Shepherd to sit again, and command him to stay.
4. After a few seconds, say "Release" and reward him. Repeat this procedure several times.
5. You can practice this trick with your Bergamasco Shepherd several times a day, prolonging the time he stays at one spot.

How did you get on? *What challenges did you face & how did you overcome them?* What could you do better for next time? **Any new discoveries?** Funny moments? *Memorable Photos?* **Sketches?**

Any other thoughts, comments or feedback

Come

This trick teaches your Bergamasco Shepherd to come to you when you command him to.

1. Stand by your Bergamasco Shepherd, say the command you will use for this trick, for instance "Come" or "Here", praise and give him a treat. Repeat this procedure throughout the day, rewarding your Bergamasco Shepherd with different treats.
2. Walk away from your Bergamasco Shepherd and say the command you used in Step 1.
3. When he comes to you to get the reward, give him a lot of praise and treats.

How did you get on? *What challenges did you face & how did you overcome them?* What could you do better for next time? **Any new discoveries?** Funny moments? *Memorable Photos?* **Sketches?**

Any other thoughts, comments or feedback

Stand Up

This trick teaches your Bergamasco Shepherd to stand up when he is lying or sitting.

1. Make your Bergamasco Shepherd lay or sit down.
2. When he stands up on his own, give him a reward. Repeat this as long as it is needed for your Bergamasco Shepherd to learn that what brings him a reward is standing up.
3. Now when your pup has made a connection between the treat and standing up, have him lying or sitting down.
4. Tell him the command "Stand" and make a gesture with your hand to give him a visual cue.
5. When he reacts correctly, reward and praise him. Even if he appears to hesitate in standing up, give him a reward to encourage him.

How did you get on? *What challenges did you face & how did you overcome them?* What could you do better for next time? **Any new discoveries?** Funny moments? *Memorable Photos?* **Sketches?**

Any other thoughts, comments or feedback

Hush!

This trick teaches your Bergamasco Shepherd to hush or stop barking when commanded.

1. Wait for your Bergamasco Shepherd to bark.
2. Look at him and if he stops barking when he notices that you are looking at him, give him a treat. Repeat this step a few times.
3. You can now start to introduce the command "Hush" before giving him a treat.
4. As your Bergamasco Shepherd gradually progresses with this trick, give him the command "Hush" while he is barking. If he stops barking, give him a treat.
5. Gradually prolong the time he should be silent after being given the command. You can also introduce a hand signal that he will associate with the command and the required behavior.

How did you get on? *What challenges did you face & how did you overcome them?* What could you do better for next time? **Any new discoveries?** Funny moments? *Memorable Photos?* **Sketches?**

Any other thoughts, comments or feedback

Walk With Me

These steps will teach your Bergamasco Shepherd to walk by your side.

1. Have your Bergamasco Shepherd on a leash walk by your side. If he pulls away, do not follow him in that direction.
2. Whenever your Bergamasco Shepherd walks close to you, give him a treat.
3. When he starts walking by your side without pulling away, introduce the command "With Me" or "Walk with Me". He will eventually begin to associate the command with walking close to you.
4. After ten steps of walking by your side, give your Bergamasco Shepherd a treat. You can practice this trick 4-5 times a day.
5. When your Bergamasco Shepherd becomes familiar with the command, and responds to it appropriately, you can start training him without his leash.

How did you get on? *What challenges did you face & how did you overcome them?* What could you do better for next time? **Any new discoveries?** Funny moments? *Memorable Photos?* **Sketches?**

Any other thoughts, comments or feedback

Kiss Me

These steps will teach your Bergamasco Shepherd to kiss you on your cheek through a pecking motion.

1. Sit in front of your Bergamasco Shepherd.
2. Hold the treat in front of your head and say "Kiss".
3. When your Bergamasco Shepherd moves towards you to take the treat, quickly offer him your cheek for him to touch it and quickly pull away from him.
4. Reward your Bergamasco Shepherd and give him the treat.
5. Gradually introduce the command "Kiss" each time your Bergamasco Shepherd pecks your cheek.
6. Repeat this training session until your Bergamasco Shepherd performs the trick on command.

How did you get on? *What challenges did you face & how did you overcome them?* What could you do better for next time? **Any new discoveries?** Funny moments? *Memorable Photos?* **Sketches?**

Any other thoughts, comments or feedback

Say Hello

This will teach your Bergamasco Shepherd to come to you and place his head on your knees.

1. For this trick, you have to sit on a chair or sofa.
2. Take a treat and place your hand between your knees.
3. When your Bergamasco Shepherd gets close to you and touches your leg, say the command "Say hello". Do not give the treat to him yet.
4. The next step is to say "Ok" to release your pup, and when he removes his head and is no longer touching your leg, give him the reward.
5. As you train your Bergamasco Shepherd, try to prolong the time he is touching your leg or keeping his head on your knees.

How did you get on? *What challenges did you face & how did you overcome them?* What could you do better for next time? **Any new discoveries?** Funny moments? *Memorable Photos?* **Sketches?**

Any other thoughts, comments or feedback

Shake Hands

Your Bergamasco Shepherd will offer his paw to you upon command.

1. Have your Bergamasco Shepherd sit facing you.
2. Then say "Shake hands" and take his paw, showing him what to do.
3. Hold his paw for a couple of seconds and give him a treat. Repeat this several times a day.
4. Check how your Bergamasco Shepherd is progressing with his training from time to time. To do this, tell him to "shake hands", and do not take his paw but let him give you his paw himself. If he still does not react to your cue, continue taking him through steps 1 to 3 until he has mastered this trick.

How did you get on? *What challenges did you face & how did you overcome them?* What could you do better for next time? **Any new discoveries?** Funny moments? *Memorable Photos?* **Sketches?**

Any other thoughts, comments or feedback

High Five

Your Bergamasco Shepherd will sit and raise his paw to tap your hand.

1. First command your Bergamasco Shepherd to sit and give him the treat.
2. While he is sitting, take another treat and hold it in front of him but out of his reach.
3. When your Bergamasco Shepherd lifts his paw to grab the treat, tap his paw with your hand, saying the command "High Five" and reward him immediately.
4. If your Bergamasco Shepherd does not respond to the treat and does not want to lift his paw and grab it, gently tap the inside of his knee. When he bends the leg, tickle the bottom of his paw to make him lift his leg.

How did you get on? *What challenges did you face & how did you overcome them?* What could you do better for next time? **Any new discoveries?** Funny moments? *Memorable Photos?* **Sketches?**

Any other thoughts, comments or feedback

Peek-A-Boo

Your Bergamasco Shepherd will raise his paw in front of his eyes as if covering them.

1. Have your Bergamasco Shepherd sit in front of you and command him to give you his paw.
2. When he does this, take his paw and gently raise it over his eyes.
3. Say the command "Peek-a-boo" and give him a treat.
4. Repeat these steps several times allowing your Bergamasco Shepherd to make a connection between the command and action.

How did you get on? *What challenges did you face & how did you overcome them?* What could you do better for next time? **Any new discoveries?** Funny moments? *Memorable Photos?* **Sketches?**

Any other thoughts, comments or feedback

Catch!

These steps will teach your Bergamasco Shepherd to catch treats, balls or other items.

1. Stand close to your Bergamasco Shepherd.
2. Throw him a treat.
3. If he catches the treat, praise him and give him another treat. If your pup misses the treat, take the treat away and try again.
4. Repeat this until he performs well.
5. Now is the time to introduce the command "Catch". Say "Catch" and throw a treat to your Bergamasco Shepherd.
6. Reward him when he catches the treat.

How did you get on? *What challenges did you face & how did you overcome them?* What could you do better for next time? **Any new discoveries?** Funny moments? *Memorable Photos?* **Sketches?**

Any other thoughts, comments or feedback

Learn Names

This trick will teach your Bergamasco Shepherd the names of some common things he finds in his surroundings

1. Offer your Bergamasco Shepherd an open-hand gesture to have him touch it.
2. When he touches your hand, give him a treat.
3. Take an object that you want to teach the name of to your Bergamasco Shepherd and hold it in your hand.
4. Say "Touch" and when he touches the object, reward him. Do not reward your Bergamasco Shepherd if he touches your hand instead of the object.
5. Repeat again, but this time when he touches the object, say the name of the object and give him a treat.
6. Repeat these training steps several times.
7. Now, hold the object, say the name of the object and when he touches it, reward him.

How did you get on? *What challenges did you face & how did you overcome them?* What could you do better for next time? **Any new discoveries?** Funny moments? *Memorable Photos?* **Sketches?**

Any other thoughts, comments or feedback

Take It!

Teach your Bergamasco Shepherd to pick up a toy or any other item.

1. Place one of your pup's toys on the ground.
2. When he touches the toy and picks it up in his mouth, give him a treat.
3. Repeat this several times until he picks up the toy immediately.
4. Now introduce the command "Take it". When he picks up the toy on his own, say the command and give him a treat.
5. Repeat this several times and practice this trick in sessions until he picks up the toy at your command.
6. When your Bergamasco Shepherd is familiar with this command, try to use the command for picking up other items.
7. To practice this, point to a ball, shoe, or anything else and command "Take it" and reward him if he performs it well.

How did you get on? *What challenges did you face & how did you overcome them?* What could you do better for next time? **Any new discoveries?** Funny moments? *Memorable Photos?* **Sketches?**

Any other thoughts, comments or feedback

Leave It!

This teaches your Bergamasco Shepherd to leave an item or to not pick it up.

1. Have your Bergamasco Shepherd on a leash.
2. Drop a few treats in front of him. When he starts reaching for the treat, pull him back with your leash and say his name, followed by the command "Leave it".
3. When he looks at you, give him a treat. This treat should be better than the one you dropped in front of him originally.
4. When he takes the treat you gave him, praise him.
5. Repeat this training session several times. You can vary the treats but the one you are rewarding your Bergamasco Shepherd with should be better than the one he has to leave.
6. As your Bergamasco Shepherd progresses with mastering this trick, you can train him off leash in a fenced area.
7. You can also start calling him away from other dogs. Then, when he reacts positively to your command, praise him and let him go back.

How did you get on? *What challenges did you face & how did you overcome them?* What could you do better for next time? **Any new discoveries?** Funny moments? *Memorable Photos?* **Sketches?**

Any other thoughts, comments or feedback

Fetch

This trick teaches your Bergamasco Shepherd to fetch you a ball or any other item.

1. Take a tennis ball or any other rubber ball that is not too large for your Bergamasco Shepherd.
2. Make an incision in the ball so that you can place some treats inside it.
3. When you start teaching your Bergamasco Shepherd this trick, show him the ball and the treats inside.
4. Then, take one treat from the ball and give it to him so that he sees where the treats are coming from.
5. Throw the ball and say "Fetch".
6. In the beginning, run together with your Bergamasco Shepherd to get the ball.
7. When he catches the ball, give him another treat from the ball.
8. As you progress with the training, you will give less treats to your Bergamasco Shepherd, so that eventually you are relying solely on the command "Fetch" for him to perform the trick.

How did you get on? *What challenges did you face & how did you overcome them?* What could you do better for next time? **Any new discoveries?** Funny moments? *Memorable Photos?* **Sketches?**

Any other thoughts, comments or feedback

Pick Up The Toys

Your Bergamasco Shepherd will be able to pick up his toys and put them back in his toy basket.

1. Place your pup's toys-filled basket in front of you.
2. Take one toy and throw it away.
3. When he chases after it and grabs it, take a treat and hold it above the basket.
4. Ideally, he will come to you, with the toy in his mouth.
5. Command him to release the toy.
6. If he reacts to the command and performs the trick, give him the treat and a lot of praise. If your Bergamasco Shepherd does not come to you with the toy in his mouth, hide the treat and command him to fetch.
7. When he takes the toy, show him the treat again, holding it above the basket.

How did you get on? *What challenges did you face & how did you overcome them?* What could you do better for next time? **Any new discoveries?** Funny moments? *Memorable Photos?* **Sketches?** Any other thoughts, comments or feedback

Find It!

With this trick you will teach your Bergamasco Shepherd to find different items.

1. Command your Bergamasco Shepherd to sit.
2. Show him an object he knows and let him smell it.
3. Hide the object under some nearby furniture, so that he sees where you place the object.
4. Give the command "Find it". If he knows the name of the object, you can add the name of the object after the command.
5. When he touches the object, give him a treat.
6. Repeat this training session several times but hide the object at different locations.
7. When your Bergamasco Shepherd gets accustomed to this and reacts immediately to your command, hide some objects he is not familiar with and give the "Find it" command. It is important to first let him smell the objects you hide.

How did you get on? *What challenges did you face & how did you overcome them?* What could you do better for next time? **Any new discoveries?** Funny moments? *Memorable Photos?* **Sketches?**

Any other thoughts, comments or feedback

Bring The Leash

This trick teaches your Bergamasco Shepherd to bring his leash to you.

1. Lay the leash on the floor.
2. Command him to take the leash.
3. Give your Bergamasco Shepherd a treat when he obeys.
4. Now go to the door.
5. Tell him to take the leash and command him to bring it and drop it in your hand.
6. Repeat these steps several times and introduce the command "Leash" when he drops the leash in your hands.
7. When your Bergamasco Shepherd gets accustomed to this cue, command him to take the leash only with the command "leash".

How did you get on? *What challenges did you face & how did you overcome them?* What could you do better for next time? **Any new discoveries?** Funny moments? *Memorable Photos?* **Sketches?**

Any other thoughts, comments or feedback

Roll Over

This trick will teach your Bergamasco Shepherd to lie down and roll over.

1. To perform this trick, make your Bergamasco Shepherd lie on his tummy.
2. You have to kneel behind or stand over him.
3. Take a treat and hold it near his nose but don't give it to him.
4. Now, you will use this treat to make your Bergamasco Shepherd roll over. Move the treat in one side, making a circular movement so that he moves to his side and rolls over.
5. When he rolls over, give him the treat.

Tip: *You may not succeed in making your Bergamasco Shepherd roll over at first, but even if you just managed to get him on his side, you are on the right track. Continue to refine by repeating.*

How did you get on? *What challenges did you face & how did you overcome them?* What could you do better for next time? **Any new discoveries?** Funny moments? *Memorable Photos?* **Sketches?**

Any other thoughts, comments or feedback

Dance

Your Bergamasco Shepherd will stand on his hind legs and spin.

1. Command your Bergamasco Shepherd to sit.
2. Hold a treat above his head to make him stand up and lift his head to smell the treat.
3. When he rises to his hind legs and maintains his balance, move the treat around his head to make him dance or spin.

Note: *Be wary of your Bergamasco Shepherd not losing his balance during these steps.*

How did you get on? *What challenges did you face & how did you overcome them?* What could you do better for next time? **Any new discoveries?** Funny moments? *Memorable Photos?* **Sketches?**

Any other thoughts, comments or feedback

Walk Backwards

This trick teaches your Bergamasco Shepherd to move backwards

1. Call him to come to you.
2. Command him to stay.
3. Move a few steps from him, stop and say the command "Back".
4. Walk towards your Bergamasco Shepherd repeating the command.
5. When he makes a few steps back, give him a treat.
6. If he does not back away, come close to him and nudge him gently with your legs.
7. If he is still not reacting to your command, hold a treat slightly behind his back to encourage him to walk back.

Tip: *If your Bergamasco Shepherd tries to turn around instead of walking back, practice this trick in an enclosed space so that he cannot turn around.*

How did you get on? *What challenges did you face & how did you overcome them?* What could you do better for next time? **Any new discoveries?** Funny moments? *Memorable Photos?* **Sketches?**

Any other thoughts, comments or feedback

Slalom

Your Bergamasco Shepherd will move between slalom poles.

Tip 1: *Use dog training slalom poles because these are designed specifically for dog training and are less likely to injure your Bergamasco Shepherd.*
Tip 2: *Use only 4-5 poles. You will increase the number of poles later.*

1. Place the poles at equal distances between each other.
2. Hold a treat in front of your pup's nose. Move the treat between the poles, encouraging him to follow. Do not rush. Move slowly so that he can follow you.
3. When he reaches the end and passes the poles, give him the treat and praise him.
4. As your Bergamasco Shepherd gets accustomed to this trick, and confidence grows, add more poles.

How did you get on? *What challenges did you face & how did you overcome them?* What could you do better for next time? **Any new discoveries?** Funny moments? *Memorable Photos?* **Sketches?**

Any other thoughts, comments or feedback

Army Crawl

Your Bergamasco Shepherd will lie down and crawl.

1. Have your Bergamasco Shepherd lie down.
2. Take his favorite treat and hold it in front of him but hold it firmly not allowing him to take it.
3. When he has smelled the treat, start dragging the treat along the floor and when he begins to follow you and crawl along the floor, reward him with the treat.
4. Every time you try this trick with your Bergamasco Shepherd, let him crawl a bit longer before giving him a reward.
5. If he tries to stand up to take the treat, take the treat away from him and start the trick again, right from the start.

How did you get on? *What challenges did you face & how did you overcome them?* What could you do better for next time? **Any new discoveries?** Funny moments? *Memorable Photos?* **Sketches?**

Any other thoughts, comments or feedback

Take a Bow

This trick teaches your Bergamasco Shepherd to bow when commanded. He will place his head on the floor while keeping his rear up.

Method 1

1. Wait for your Bergamasco Shepherd to take a big stretch with his head near the floor.
2. When he does this, say "Take a Bow".
3. As always, give your Bergamasco Shepherd a reward. If you use this command almost every time your pup does this stretch, he will learn to react to the command.

Tip: *If you choose this method to teach your Bergamasco Shepherd how to take a bow, you have to be patient because in some cases, it may take several months to learn this trick.*

How did you get on? *What challenges did you face & how did you overcome them?* What could you do better for next time? **Any new discoveries?** Funny moments? *Memorable Photos?* **Sketches?**

Any other thoughts, comments or feedback

Method 2

1. First, prepare a treat and have your Bergamasco Shepherd prepared in a standing position.
2. Hold the treat near the floor so that he reaches for it. Be ready to hold your hand below his belly to keep his rear end up and prevent him from lying down.
3. When in the right position, say "Take a Bow" and keep him in that position for a few seconds.
4. Release him (say "Ok" or "Release") and give him the reward.

Tip: *The second method is slightly more direct and it may take less time to teach your Bergamasco Shepherd to take a bow.*

How did you get on? *What challenges did you face & how did you overcome them?* What could you do better for next time? **Any new discoveries?** Funny moments? *Memorable Photos?* **Sketches?**

Any other thoughts, comments or feedback

Take a Nap

Your Bergamasco Shepherd will lie down on the floor as if taking a nap.

1. First, make your Bergamasco Shepherd lie down on his belly. If you have a hard time making him do this, you can lure him into this position with a treat. Do not give him the treat when he is already lying down.
2. Roll him over to his side, but do this carefully as you don't want to make your pup nervous.
3. While he is lying on his side with his head on the floor, tell him to "Take a Nap".
4. Repeat the command, making sure that he stays in this position for a couple of seconds.
5. Then say "Wake up" and let your Bergamasco Shepherd stand up.
6. Give him a reward for doing the trick.

How did you get on? *What challenges did you face & how did you overcome them?* What could you do better for next time? **Any new discoveries?** Funny moments? *Memorable Photos?* **Sketches?**

Any other thoughts, comments or feedback

Leaping Over Objects

This trick teaches your Bergamasco Shepherd to leap over objects.

1. Command your Bergamasco Shepherd to sit and stay.
2. Lay a stick on the ground and stand facing him.
3. Call him to come to you.
4. When he crosses the stick, praise him and give him a treat.
5. Repeat these steps a few more times.
6. Lift the stick just a few inches off the floor. You can use two alphabet blocks or any other solid objects to raise the stick. The stick should be just high enough that your Bergamasco Shepherd can still cross it without jumping.
7. Call him to you, and when he crosses the stick, give him a treat.
8. Repeat this session a few more times until confidence grows.
9. Next, raise the stick higher so that he now needs to jump to cross it.
10. Call him and when he jumps, say the command "Leap" and give your Bergamasco Shepherd a treat.
11. Train him until he performs the trick when commanded.

How did you get on? *What challenges did you face & how did you overcome them?* What could you do better for next time? **Any new discoveries?** Funny moments? *Memorable Photos?* **Sketches?**

Any other thoughts, comments or feedback

Play Soccer

Your pup will dribble a ball.

Tip: *For this trick, use a larger ball so that your Bergamasco Shepherd cannot take it in his mouth and carry it around.*

1. Take your Bergamasco Shepherd to some open space.
2. Give him the ball and leave him to get familiar with it. It may be that he just smells the ball, try to carry it or touch it with his paws. If your Bergamasco Shepherd behaves in this manner, praise him but do not give him any treats yet.
3. If he does not show any interest in the ball, roll the ball towards him and try to engage him in playing with the ball.
4. Give your Bergamasco Shepherd a treat whenever he touches the ball with his paw or nose or starts to roll the ball.
5. Repeat this practice encouraging him to roll the ball a bit longer and eventually, he will get the hang of dribbling the ball.
6. Give a reward to your Bergamasco Shepherd whenever he dribbles the ball.

How did you get on? *What challenges did you face & how did you overcome them?* What could you do better for next time? **Any new discoveries?** Funny moments? *Memorable Photos?* **Sketches?**

Any other thoughts, comments or feedback

Settle Down

There may be times when you need your Bergamasco Shepherd to calm down and relax for some time. The value of teaching the "settle down" trick is that you'll get to choose when you want him to be calm and relax.

1. Training your Bergamasco Shepherd to settle down should start from the beginning. Use a leash on your puppy and have him settle down; this can take five minutes or as long as half an hour.

2. As he does this, tell him to "Settle down" so that he gets used to hearing it while he is relaxed and calm. Early on in his life he must be taught that it isn't all about play and that both of you need your quiet moments.

3. As he is tied to the leash, he is allowed to lie down on his front or back, and even stretch out. Take advantage of this trick by practicing it throughout the day. For example when you are about to cook, reading the newspaper, or when you are watching television. In the beginning you may experience your Bergamasco Shepherd being vocal about his dislike for the leash. After a few days he will become accustomed to it.

Notes: While practicing this trick in the beginning, keep your pup close to you. After a few days, put him in a different room, or slightly farther as long as you are out of his sight. This is a good time to incorporate the "Go to" command as you teach him to go to his crate, mat, or kennel then follow it up with "Settle down". For example, tell him to go to his crate as you lead him there using a food treat which he receives as soon as he obeys your command. Take advantage of the fact that young puppies are able to absorb place tricks quicker than older dogs. If his mat is kept at the same location consistently, he will learn "go to mat" in just a few days. Crates, mats, and kennels are useful because they are portable. If you travel often this command will be extremely helpful.

When you begin taking your Bergamasco Shepherd outside on walks, practice the "settle down" command in public places such as parks. While walking, stop at the corner of a street and ask him to settle down. Wait a few minutes before proceeding with your walk. Teaching your pup to have quiet moments outdoors where he would typically get excited is an effective way of training him how to settle down regardless of all the distractions.

As you practice the "settle down" trick while taking your pup out for a walk, try to keep it fun for him. Keep in mind that having him settle down for 10 minutes at a time is fine; just don't overdo it.

How did you get on? *What challenges did you face & how did you overcome them?* What could you do better for next time? **Any new discoveries?** Funny moments? *Memorable Photos?* **Sketches?**

Any other thoughts, comments or feedback

Stay

"Stay" may seem like a similar command to "Settle down", but they are two different tricks with their own benefits. Settle down is used when you want your Bergamasco Shepherd to quietly wait in one location in a position that is comfortable for him. On the other hand, a command to "stay" means you are instructing him to remain in a specific position. Both of these commands are very useful for every owner. When choosing which one to use, keep in mind that "settle down" is used for extended periods of time whereas "stay" is just for a few minutes.

It is important to ensure your Bergamasco Shepherd fully understands the "Settle down" command for him to efficiently learn "stay" and other similar obedience tricks. The foundation of successfully teaching the stay command is based on the following:

a) Use short stays in the beginning so that your pup has higher chances of succeeding;

b) Generously handing out treats when he stays in the correct position

c) To start, instruct him to stay for just five minutes. Once he succeeds, immediately reward him with treats. Gradually increase the duration of his stays but be careful not to push him too hard. This will lead to frustration on your part and it will only feel like punishment for your pup.

d) While it may seem that your Bergamasco Shepherd isn't doing much when he obeys the stay command, he is restraining himself from movement. This kind of positive behavior should be rewarded immediately in puppies especially because it is an achievement in itself. Be generous with praise, petting, and rewards to communicate to him that he is doing a good job.

e) Give regular feedback during the process of training him how to stay. Use this phrase: "good – stay – his name". This kind of verbalization will tell your Bergamasco Shepherd three key things:

1. "Good" continuously informs him that he is doing the right thing. As mentioned earlier, praise during training is crucial whenever he gets it right. This is the only way he will know the difference between performing the right or wrong action.

2. "Stay" is a word used by everyone, but when you address it to your puppy together with "good" and his name - this avoids confusion. Be firm but not tough, use an affectionate and kind voice when commanding him. In fact once your Bergamasco Shepherd is well-trained he will obey commands even if you use whispers.

3. Using his name when instructing various commands will let him know that the request was made for him. Use it throughout your training as it also calls his attention.

How did you get on? *What challenges did you face & how did you overcome them?* What could you do better for next time? **Any new discoveries?** Funny moments? *Memorable Photos?* **Sketches?**

Any other thoughts, comments or feedback

Down

Teaching your Bergamasco Shepherd the "down" command can be done as soon as he has mastered the "sit" command.

1. While your pup is sitting, instruct him to go "down" by having him sniff a food treat while lowering it to the ground and placing it between his forepaws while you are still holding it.
2. Slowly move the treat backwards towards his chest or forward away from his paws to encourage him to lie down.
3. As soon as he lies down, immediately reward him with the treat.

Teaching the "down" command can also be done while your puppy is standing.

1. Instruct him "down" as you lower a food lure to the ground between his fore paws.
2. As soon as he lowers his head, move the treat backwards towards his forelegs, forcing his rump to collapse eventually making him lie down.
3. If your Bergamasco Shepherd backs up instead of lying down, practice this command in a corner. Keep in mind that the "down" command requires extra patience from your part because it is the most challenging of the body-position change tricks.

How did you get on? *What challenges did you face & how did you overcome them?* What could you do better for next time? **Any new discoveries?** Funny moments? *Memorable Photos?* **Sketches?**

Any other thoughts, comments or feedback

Dog Walking

As your puppy grows, exercise should be a regular part of his life - especially as he will naturally be active and so should be walked daily. Follow these simple steps to learn how to effectively walk your Bergamasco Shepherd:

1. As you walk, always stay in front of him. Doing this early on will teach him to see you as the pack leader; whereas if you let him walk in front of you, he will assume the pack leader role.
2. You should be the first one to step out of the door as you leave for a walk, and be the first one in.
3. During the walk, he should stay by your side if not behind you.
4. Short leashes allow you to have more control. Place it on the top of his neck which will be more effective as you communicate with him during the walk. Use the leash to guide where your Bergamasco Shepherd should be.
4. Set aside 30 minutes to an hour per day for your dog walk. However, keep in mind that each Bergamasco Shepherd has different needs. If you aren't sure, you can always consult your vet.

How did you get on? *What challenges did you face & how did you overcome them?* What could you do better for next time? **Any new discoveries?** Funny moments? *Memorable Photos?* **Sketches?**

Any other thoughts, comments or feedback

Heel

Teaching your Bergamasco Shepherd how to heel will train him to stay on either side of you (left hand side in these steps) as you go for your walks. This command can come in handy whether or not you are using a leash. For this trick, have a handful of treats and spoon with some wet dog food or peanut butter ready on it.

1. Start by having your Bergamasco Shepherd sitting on your left side.

2. Hold some treats or the spoonful of peanut butter on your left hand, facing your pup's nose then give the command "heel".

3. Begin walking a few steps as you gradually dole out treats.

4. When you are able to walk farther with your Bergamasco Shepherd as you give out treats, this is your cue to minimize the amount of treats so he gets used to the command.

4. Start practicing again with him sitting on your left side then asking him to heel.

5. Hand him one treat as you take a step forward, before giving him another one.

6. Make sure that you are walking short distances first and then work it up to longer distances until you reach 2 yards between treats.

7. When you succeed in walking several yards while your Bergamasco Shepherd is in heel as you use a few treats, this is your cue to wean him off the treats during the heel command. You may continue giving them, just a few treats at a time.

8. Be observant of your pup; if he comes out of heel this may be a sign that you are moving too fast for him.

As you progress in training the heel command, keep in mind that it is common for some Bergamasco Shepherds to get out of the heel position when they are just beginning to learn it. When this happens simply go back a few steps to where they were last in heel. This usually happens when we tend to move much faster in the process before he is ready.

How did you get on? *What challenges did you face & how did you overcome them?* What could you do better for next time? **Any new discoveries?** Funny moments? *Memorable Photos?* **Sketches?**

Any other thoughts, comments or feedback

Look

The "look" command is useful in getting the attention of your Bergamasco Shepherd. It will come in handy during various occasions throughout obedience training as well as when you are trying to teach him other tricks. Additionally, the "look" command is effective in treating behavioral problems because you can use it to divert his attention when he is engaging in bad behavior.

1. Make sure that you are training your Bergamasco Shepherd in a quiet, peaceful location where there is minimal to zero distractions.
2. Say your Bergamasco Shepherd's name followed by the command "look".
3. Most cooperate once they hear you say their name but if your pup looks at you upon hearing this command, use the clicker and give him a treat.
4. If your Bergamasco Shepherd doesn't respond with the "look" command, hold a treat in front of his nose as you pull it up to your face.
5. He should follow the treat then will eventually look at you. Once he does this, use the clicker accompanied by praising and rewarding with a treat.

How did you get on? *What challenges did you face & how did you overcome them?* What could you do better for next time? **Any new discoveries?** Funny moments? *Memorable Photos?* **Sketches?**

Any other thoughts, comments or feedback

The Amazing Target Stick

This section will help you greatly with teaching the more complicated tricks. The stick can be anything, from a flashy walking stick to an old garden cane.
During this type of routine your Bergamasco Shepherd will often carry the stick, jump over it or twist around it. The idea is to target him at the end of the stick. By doing this and strengthening it, you can then use the stick to lead your Bergamasco Shepherd into other tricks and positions. For example walking on back legs or jumping to touch the stick. Keep in mind that besides a stick, other objects can also be used for targeting - the principle remains the same.

1. Place the stick flat on the floor with a treat on the end. When your Bergamasco Shepherd touches the stick, reinforce and reward the touch with your sound and a food reward.
2. Now target your Bergamasco Shepherd to the stick as you did with the other objects earlier but this time when he is definitely targeted, pick up the stick by the other end.
3. Do this gently because you are aiming to move on from targeting static items to a moving one, the end of your stick, so you need to keep your pup's confidence up.
By building up the targeting response you will be able to use the stick in order to guide your Bergamasco Shepherd into many positions and places.

How did you get on? *What challenges did you face & how did you overcome them?* What could you do better for next time? **Any new discoveries?** Funny moments? *Memorable Photos?* **Sketches?** Any other thoughts, comments or feedback

Managing Bites

Puppies are curious by their nature and they use their mouth to explore the world around them, a behavior that we observe in babies as well. Unlike babies, puppies develop sharp teeth that can cause immense pain even during play. This kind of behavior is unwelcome and therefore should be addressed early on, otherwise it can continue as he grows and it will no longer be fun by that point.
How to effectively address and stop this behavior while your pup is still young? Read on...

Healthy Bite Manners

Stock up on toys and chew treats which you will use to substitute your hands, feet, fingers and toes whenever you want to play with him or pet him. Each time that you reach out to pet your pup, use your other hand to hold a treat and offer it to him so that he will direct his biting and chewing urges to the object rather than your hand. You could also teach your children this method.
1. Regularly switch hands that hold the toy so that he doesn't always expect it. This can help your pup jump at the treat or toy. The idea here is to change things up so he doesn't always know what to expect while teaching him positive connotations with people and petting. Practice this trick using short sessions so that your puppy becomes excited when you pet him. Keeping sessions too long may result in him switching to your hand.
2. In the event that a bad bite occurs, raise your voice when you say "Ouch" to communicate pain to your pup. You can even go as far as pretending to cry and whimper then suddenly ignore him. Do not pay him any attention until he calms down. Once he does, this is the only time you can give him a treat and be affectionate with him again.
3. Avoid hitting him if he still bites you. Be patient and remember that it will take a few days for him to understand what you are trying to teach him. By hitting him you are only causing him to be defensive and afraid of people's hands. He may end up hiding each time he sees you.
4. Last but not least, hitting may cause him to bite more to prevent you from hurting him.

How did you get on? *What challenges did you face & how did you overcome them?* What could you do better for next time? **Any new discoveries?** Funny moments? *Memorable Photos?* **Sketches?**

Any other thoughts, comments or feedback

* 9 7 8 1 5 2 6 9 4 5 8 2 2 *

SD - #0221 - 291221 - C0 - 229/152/7 - PB - 9781526945822 - Matt Lamination